My Adoptive Family

Julie Murray

Abdo Kids Junior
is an Imprint of Abdo Kids
abdobooks.com

Abdo
THIS IS MY FAMILY
Kids

abdobooks.com

Published by Abdo Kids, a division of ABDO, P.O. Box 398166, Minneapolis, Minnesota 55439. Copyright © 2021 by Abdo Consulting Group, Inc. International copyrights reserved in all countries. No part of this book may be reproduced in any form without written permission from the publisher. Abdo Kids Junior™ is a trademark and logo of Abdo Kids.

Printed in the United States of America, North Mankato, Minnesota.

052020

092020

 THIS BOOK CONTAINS
RECYCLED MATERIALS

Photo Credits: iStock, Shutterstock

Production Contributors: Teddy Borth, Jennie Forsberg, Grace Hansen

Design Contributors: Candice Keimig, Pakou Moua, Dorothy Toth

Library of Congress Control Number: 2019955579

Publisher's Cataloging-in-Publication Data

Names: Murray, Julie, author.

Title: My adoptive family / by Julie Murray

Description: Minneapolis, Minnesota : Abdo Kids, 2021 | Series: This is my family | Includes online resources and index.

Identifiers: ISBN 9781098202217 (lib. bdg.) | ISBN 9781644943892 (pbk.) | ISBN 9781098203191 (ebook) | ISBN 9781098203689 (Read-to-Me ebook)

Subjects: LCSH: Families--Juvenile literature. | Adoption--Juvenile literature. | Adopted children--Family relationships--Juvenile literature. | Parent and child--Juvenile literature. | Families--Social aspects—Juvenile literature.

Classification: DDC 306.85--dc23

Table of Contents

My Adoptive Family

Sometimes parents cannot care for a child. Out of love, they place the child with a new family.

Adoptive families are special. But they act the same as all families.

They laugh. Timmy tells a joke.

They help. Abbey helps take care of Joe.

They play. Charlie plays with her sister.

They spend time together. The family takes Oscar for a walk.

They **celebrate**. It is Sophia's birthday.

They have fun. Liam plays a game.

Most of all, they love!

Jane gets a hug.

More Adoptive Families

Glossary

adoptive
relating to adoption. Adoption is the action of legally taking another's child and raising them as your own.

celebrate
recognize a special day or happy event with gifts, a party, or activity.

Index

Abdo Kids
ONLINE
FREE! ONLINE MULTIMEDIA RESOURCES

Visit **abdokids.com** to access crafts, games, videos, and more!

Use Abdo Kids code
TMK2217
or scan this QR code!